To: _____

From: _____

Dad

Published by Sellers Publishing, Inc.
Copyright © 2010 Sellers Publishing, Inc.
Photography © 2010 Kendra Dew
All rights reserved.

Edited by Robin Haywood

161 John Roberts Road, South Portland, Maine 04106
For ordering information:
(800) 625-3386 Toll free
(207) 772-6814 Fax
Visit our Web site: www.sellerspublishing.com
E-mail: rsp@rsvp.com

ISBN: 13: 978-1-4162-0566-1

10 9 8 7 6 5 4 3 2 1

Printed and bound in China.

Dad

WHAT WOULD I DO
WITHOUT SOMEONE
LIKE YOU?

PHOTOGRAPHY BY KENDRA DEW

SELLERS
PUBLISHING

*Dad, you're always there
to give me a lift.*

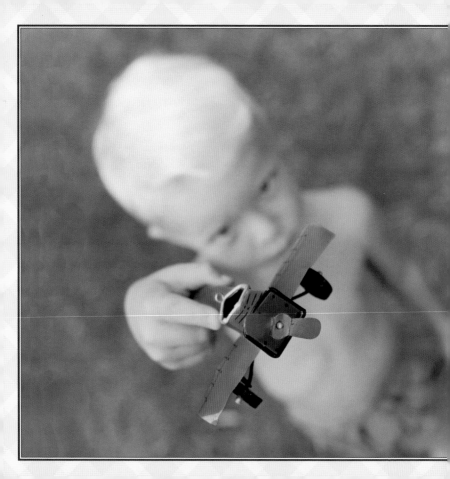

*You encouraged me
to aim for the stars*

*and taught me
to appreciate life's
simple pleasures.*

You're someone I will always look up to.

*What would we do
without you?*

*From you Dad, I discovered
the importance of joy.*

I learned that a good sense of humor is the cure for many ills

*and that laughter is
a powerful gift.*

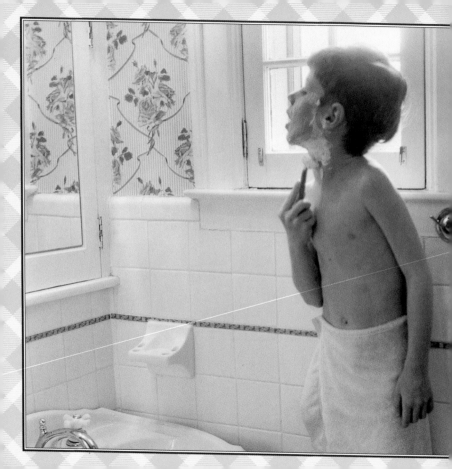

You taught me how to
be a grown-up

*and where to find
all the best stuff!*

*You prepared me for the
times ahead, and encouraged
me to find my own way.*

You said there was no place I couldn't go

and nothing I couldn't do.

Because of you,
I am happy,

and joyous,

and free.

And when the world doesn't understand me, you always do.

*I've learned the lessons of
fairness, cooperation, kindness,
and caring from you Dad,
but most of all, I learned
how to love,*

how to be gentle,

and how to appreciate nature's gifts.

*You taught me
everything I really
need to know . . .*

*like how much fun
cheap thrills can be!*

*Because of you,
I learned to like
being me.*

We know each other's hearts!

*Dad, you helped me discover
my greatest strengths,*

and taught me to meet challenges head on.